By Laura Williams
Translated by Jaspreet Kaur

© 2022 Williams Books
1 rue de l'église, 91430 Igny
Dépôt légal : Décembre 2022
ISBN 978-2-494614-56-7
Imprimé à la demande par Amazon
Loi n° 49-956 du 16 juillet 1949 sur les publications destinées à la jeunesse

ਸੌਣ ਲਈ

[saun lai] – to sleep

ਇਸ਼ਨਾਨ ਕਰਨ ਲਈ

[ishnaan karan lai] – to take a bath

ਘੁੰਮਣ ਲਈ

[ghuman lai] – to crawl

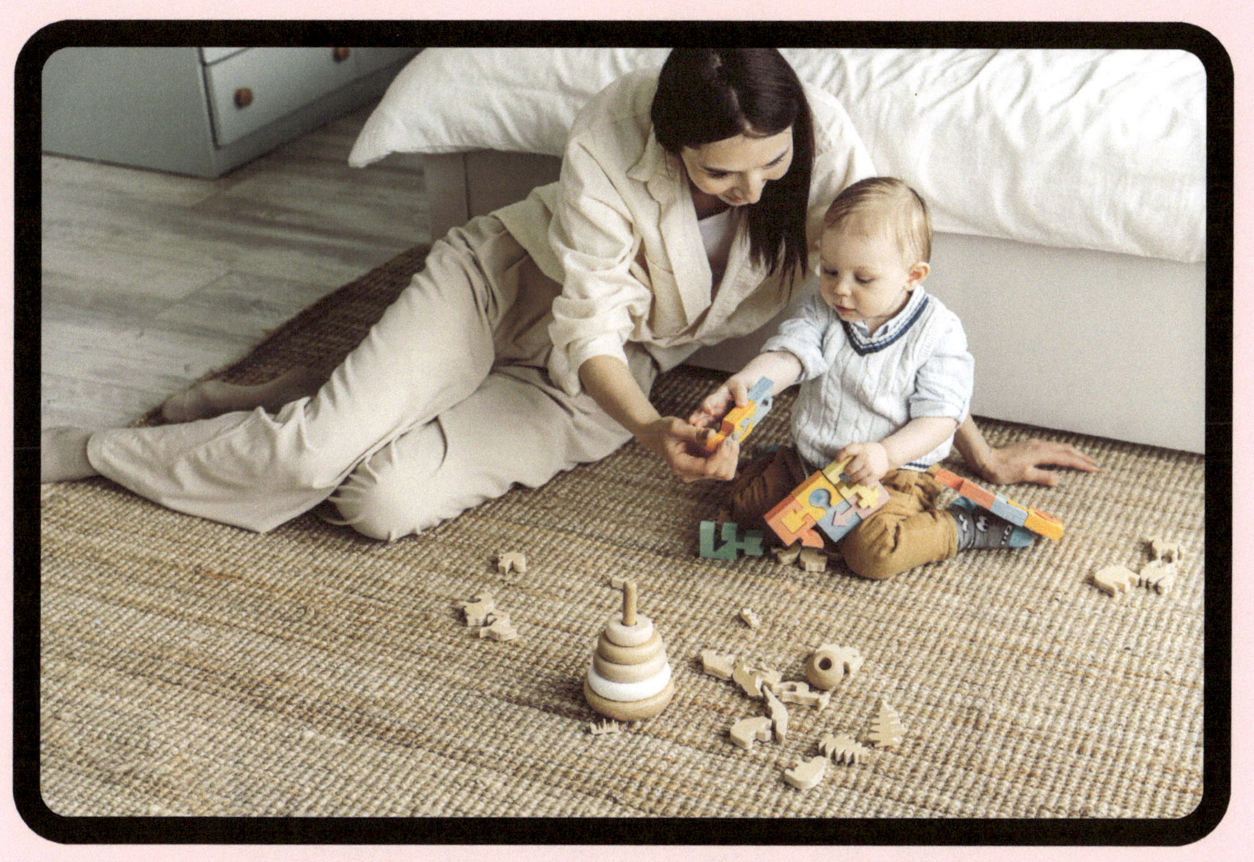

ਖੇਡਣ ਲਈ

[khedan lai] – to play

ਬੈਠਣ ਲਈ

[baitthan lai] – to sit

ਰੋਣ ਲਈ

[ron lai] - to cry

ਖੜ੍ਹੇ ਹੋਣ ਲਈ

[kharhe hon lai] – to stand

# ਤਾੜੀ ਮਾਰਨ ਲਈ

[taarhi maarana lai] - to clap

ਪੜ੍ਹਨ ਲਈ

[parhan lai] – to read

ਖਾਣ ਲਈ

[khaan lai] – to eat

ਪੀਣ ਲਈ

[peen lai] – to drink

ਹਸਣ ਲਈ

[hasan lai] - to laugh

ਜੱਫੀ ਪਾਉਣ ਲਈ

[japhi paaun lai] – to hug

ਤੁਰਨ ਲਈ

[turan lai] – to walk

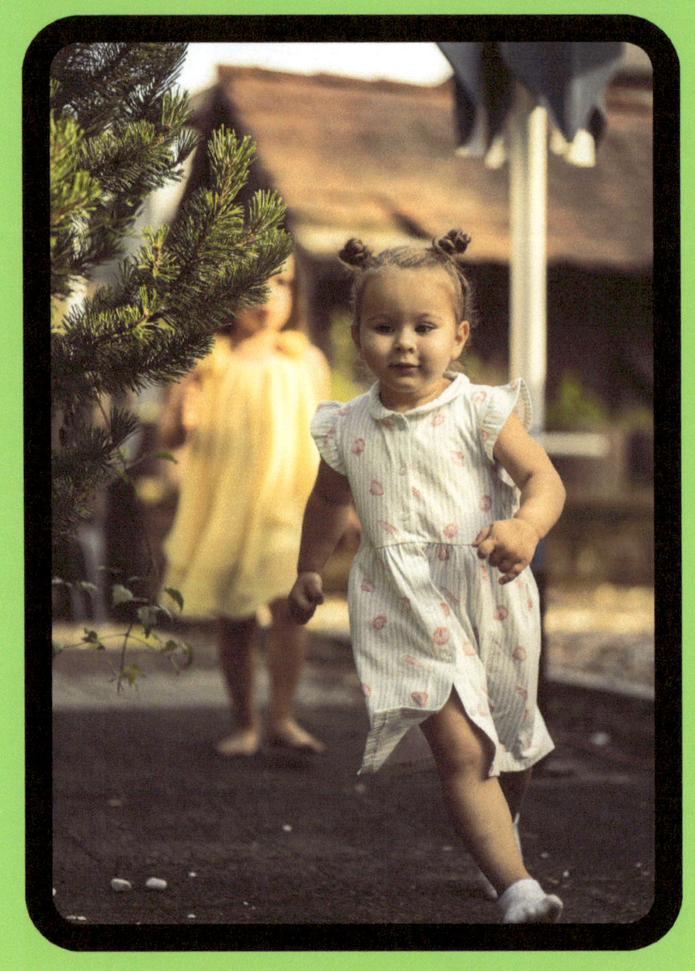

ਦੋੜਨ ਲਈ

[daudan lai] - to run

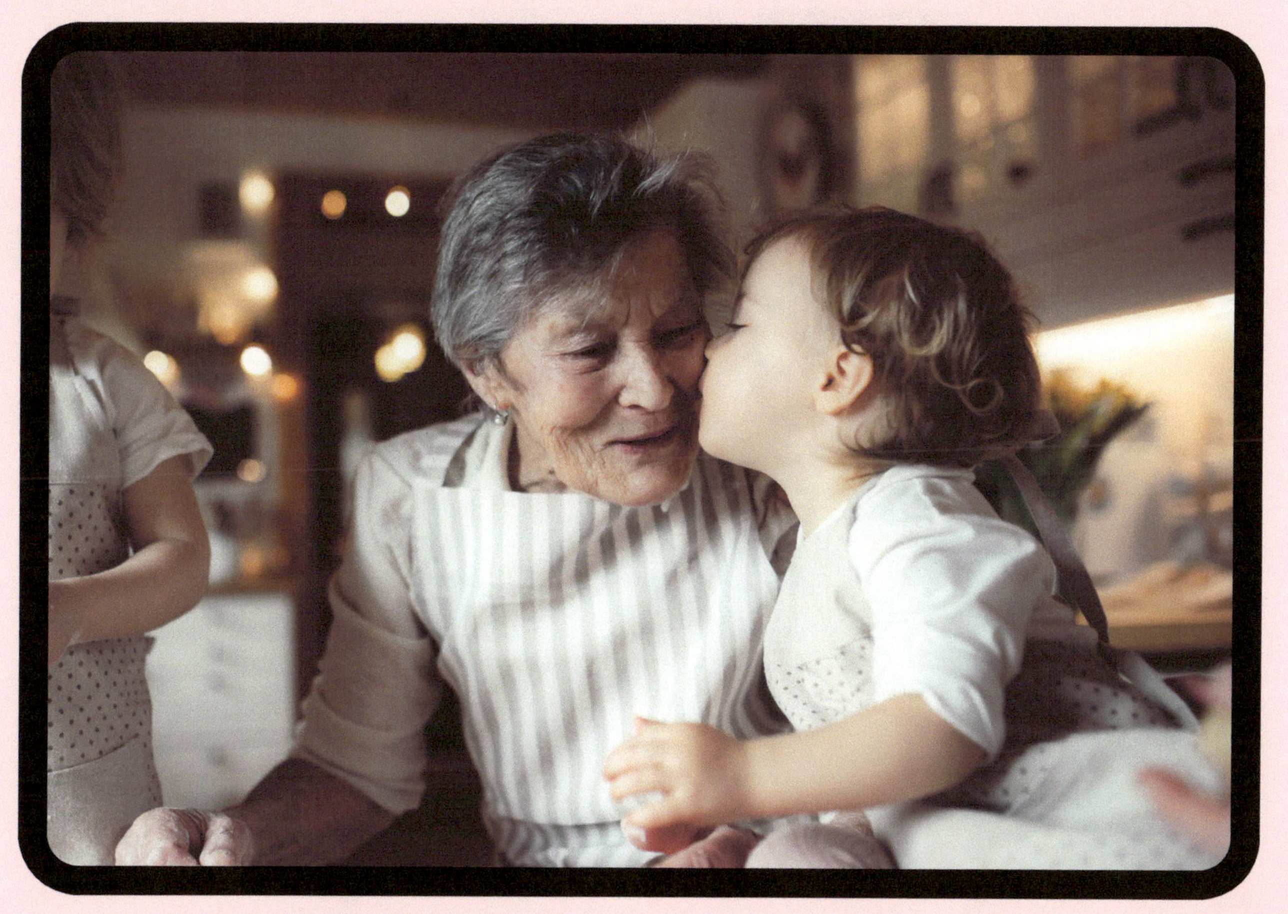

ਚੁੰਮਣ ਲਈ

[chuman lai] – to kiss

ਕੁੱਦਣ ਲਈ

[kuddan lai] - to jump

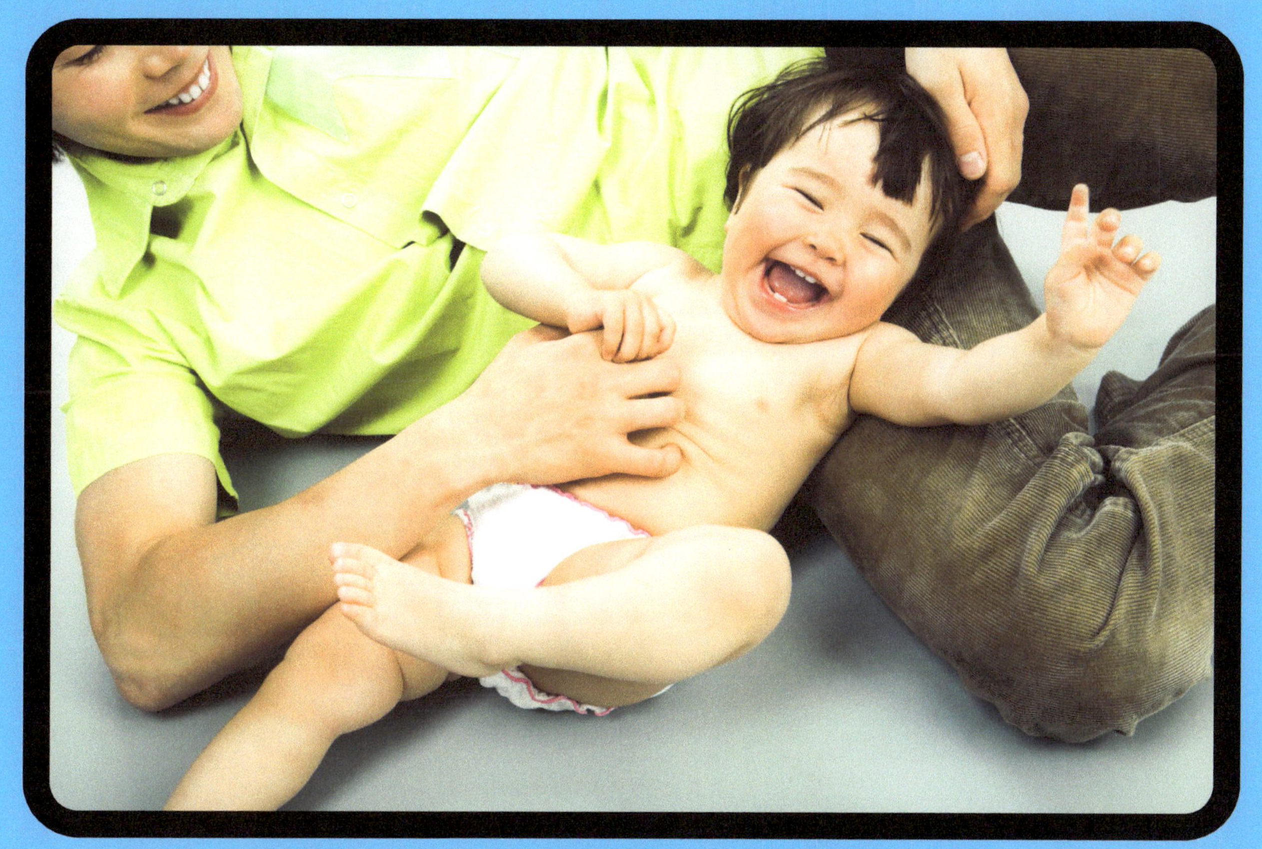

ਗੁਦਗੁਦੀ ਲਈ

[gudgudi lai] – to tickle

ਨਚਣ ਲਈ

[nachan lai] - to dance

ਪਕਾਉਣ ਲਈ

[pakaaun lai] – to cook

ਗੋਡੇ ਟੇਕਣ ਲਈ

[gode ttekan lai] – to kneel

ਢਕਣ ਲਈ

[dhakan lai] - to push

ਖਿਚਣ ਲਈ

[khichan lai] – to pull

ਲਿਖਣ ਲਈ

[likhan lai] – to write

ਗਾਉਣ ਲਈ

[gaaun lai] - to sing

Thank you

Thank you for purchasing "Punjabi-English Words for Toddlers"! Your support means a lot to me, and I hope you and your child enjoy these books.

If you have a moment, I would greatly appreciate it if you could leave a review on Amazon. Your feedback will help me improve future editions of the series and create more resources for bilingual children.

Thank you again for your support. You can access the reviews on Amazon by scanning the QR code below or by visiting the link below:

https://www.amazon.com/review/create-review?&asin=2494614562

Thank you for helping me continue my work as a language teacher and translator. Your support is greatly appreciated!

In the same collection

www.ingramcontent.com/pod-product-compliance
Lightning Source LLC
LaVergne TN
LVHW071703180726
843512LV00002B/535